CORNERSTONES OF FREEDOM™

THE SALEM WITCH TRIALS

BY PETER BENOIT

CHILDREN'S PRESS®

An Imprint of Scholastic Inc.

New York Toronto London Auckland Sydney

Mexico City New Delhi Hong Kong

Danbury, Connecticut

BRINGING HISTORY to LIFE

Content Consultant
James Marten, PhD
Professor and Chair, History Department
Marquette University
Milwaukee, Wisconsin

Library of Congress Cataloging-in-Publication Data

Benoit, Peter, 1955–
   The Salem witch trials / by Peter Benoit.
      pages cm—(Cornerstones of freedom)
   Includes bibliographical references and index.
   ISBN 978-0-531-28206-9 (lib. bdg.) — ISBN 978-0-531-27671-6 (pbk.)
   1. Trials (Witchcraft)—Massachusetts—Salem—Juvenile literature.
   I. Title.
   KFM2478.8.W5B46 2013
   345.744'50288—dc23   2013000080

1 2 3 4 5 6 7 8 9 10 R 23 22 21 20 19 18 17 16 15 14

Photographs © 2014: age fotostock/Everett Collection, Inc: back cover;
Alamy Images: 45 (Maurice Savage), 20 (Stock Montage, Inc.); AP Images:
54 (Ed Suba Jr./Akron Beacon Journal), 2, 3, 6, 11, 13, 17, 21, 22, 23, 25,
29, 30, 36, 41, 58 (North Wind Archives), 55 (William J. Smith); Bridgeman
Art Library: 18 (Look and Learn), 5 bottom, 12, 57 top (Massachusetts
Historical Society, Boston, MA, USA); Corbis Images/Bettmann: 14;
Everett Collection/7 Continents History: 4 bottom, 10; Getty Images: 5
top, 34 (Briggs Co./George Eastman House), 16 (David Q. Cavagnaro/
Peter Arnold), 51 (Evan Richman/The Boston Globe); North Wind Picture
Archives: 48; Shutterstock, Inc./HerArtSheLoves: cover; Superstock, Inc.:
24, 28, 37, 39, 42, 50 (Everett Collection), 8, 46, 57 bottom (H - D Falkenstein/
ima/imagebroker.net), 44, 56 (Universal Images Group); The Granger
Collection: 4 top, 27, 32, 38, 47; The Image Works: 7 (Ann Ronan Picture
Library/HIP), 35 (Charles Walker/Topfoto), 26 (National Maritime Museum,
London); XNR Productions, Inc.: 52, 53.

Did you know that studying history can be fun?

BRING HISTORY TO LIFE by becoming a history investigator. Examine the evidence (primary and secondary source materials); cross-examine the people and witnesses. Take a look at what was happening at the time—but be careful! What happened years ago might suddenly become incredibly interesting and change the way you think!

Contents

The Devil's Servants

Religion influenced all aspects of the Puritans' lives, and religious leaders held great power over public opinion.

The Puritans were a group of people who believed that God acted constantly in their lives. They watched carefully for signs of God's favor or disapproval in the world around them. They believed God guided them toward goodness and sometimes allowed the devil to remind them of their errors. The Puritans also believed that the devil had human servants called witches. These witches were believed to bring unthinkable mental and physical torment to those who had failed to please God.

When Puritan English immigrants settled in the Massachusetts Bay Colony in the 17th century, they brought a fear of witches with them from their homeland. Before the Salem witch trials began in early 1692, more than 80 trials for witchcraft had already occurred in New England, and hundreds of witches had been tried and executed in the previous two centuries in Europe.

Puritans believed that witches performed secret rituals and brought harm to good people.

CHAPTER 1
BEWITCHED

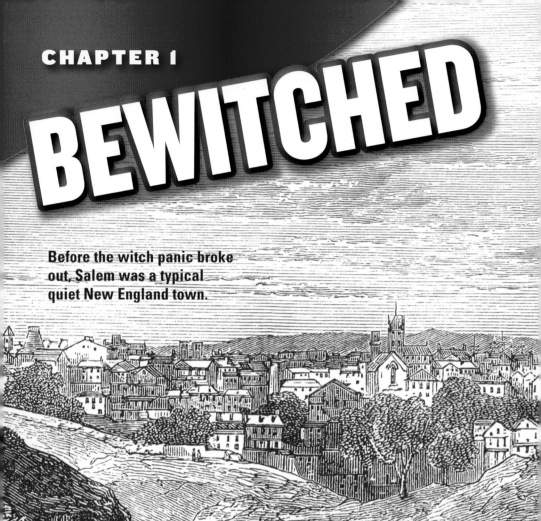

Before the witch panic broke out, Salem was a typical quiet New England town.

ON JANUARY 3, 1692, THE Reverend Samuel Parris delivered a **sermon** in which he described the devil's plot to bring down the church, aided by "wicked" people. The devil made his first appearance in Salem Village at the Reverend Parris's home. Parris's slave Tituba claimed that as she was falling asleep on January 15, a man in dark clothing appeared beside her. He forced her to sign a book promising that she would serve him for six years. The stranger then ordered her to harm Parris's daughter Elizabeth and her cousin Abigail Williams. Tituba refused. Almost immediately after the supposed encounter, Elizabeth and Abigail began to exhibit odd behaviors. Their bodies twisted, and they crouched under chairs. Abigail began to experience terrible headaches.

Rumors of Witchcraft

When the girls' **afflictions** worsened, Reverend Parris sought the advice of Salem Village's doctor, William Griggs. Griggs was unable to identify any physical injury or sickness. He concluded that Elizabeth and Abigail were under the spell of a witch. When Parris consulted other local **ministers**, they agreed with Griggs. Word spread quickly in Salem Village, and Parris's neighbors grew frightened. By late February, the villagers were strongly pressuring the girls to identify the witches who were tormenting them. Soon, the two girls accused Tituba and villagers Sarah Good and Sarah Osborn of casting spells on them.

Tituba had been Samuel Parris's slave since she was a teenager.

Afflicted people often displayed strange behaviors that disturbed devil-fearing friends and relatives in their Puritan community.

Other people soon began claiming that they were bewitched as well. Young Ann Putnam insisted that the **specter** of Sarah Good had pinched her and forced her to sign a mysterious book. Two days later, Dr. Griggs's seventeen-year-old niece Elizabeth Hubbard said that a wolf stalked her as she walked home. She believed that Sarah Good had either turned herself into the wolf or ordered a wolf to stalk her. She also said that the spirit of Sarah Osborn had harassed her, even though the elderly Osborn had difficulty moving around.

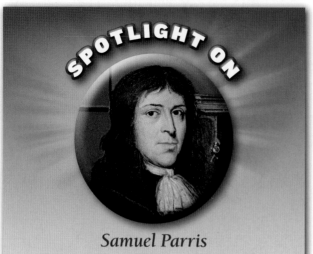

Samuel Parris

Samuel Parris was born in London, England, in 1653. He spent much of his youth in the island nation of Barbados. At the suggestion of his father, Samuel moved to Boston, Massachusetts, to study at Harvard College. When his father died in 1673, Parris left Harvard and returned to Barbados to take over his father's sugar plantation. However, the plantation was never a success, and much of it was ruined by a hurricane in 1680. After the plantation's destruction, Parris returned to Boston, where he failed as a merchant. He married Elizabeth Eldridge and moved to Salem Village, where he was hired as a minister in June 1689. Parris played a complex and controversial role in Salem's witch trials.

While it is known today that witchcraft and magic spells are not real, many people in Salem believed strongly in their existence. Some people really did consider themselves to be witches, and they attempted to perform magic. Such attempts were considered criminal acts. As a result, the accusations of witchcraft were taken very seriously by the village's people.

Suspicion Spreads

The first three women charged with witchcraft were considered outsiders by most of the other villagers. Tituba was widely believed to practice magic. Puritan ministers discouraged fortune-telling. Despite that, Tituba had once helped Parris's daughter and niece use magic to predict the identities of their future husbands. Many of Salem's Puritans believed that magic worked but that its power came from the devil. Most thought Tituba had invited the devil to Salem by performing such magic spells.

Many of the same people reasoned that Sarah Good was a witch. She was very poor and earned money by begging. People believed that she had strayed from God's word because she no longer went to church.

Because Tituba confessed to practicing witchcraft, she was never put on trial.

The people of Salem paid close attention to the events surrounding the witch trials, and news traveled quickly when someone was arrested for witchcraft.

The town gossiped about Sarah Osborn because she married her servant after her first husband died. This marriage resulted in Osborn's sons from her first marriage being denied their rightful **inheritance**. Many blamed Osborn for her children's misfortune.

The suffering of the afflicted girls worsened. Elizabeth and Abigail reported seeing Osborn turn into a bird. Ann Putnam claimed that Osborn and Tituba tried to cut off her head. Tituba, Osborn, and Good were soon arrested and brought to Nathaniel Ingersoll's tavern for questioning.

Caught in a Snare

News of the arrests spread quickly. **Magistrates** Jonathan Corwin and John Hathorne traveled to Salem Village to question the women. The villagers made their way to the tavern to observe. Giles Corey, nearing 80 years old, rode his horse to Salem Village even after his wife, Martha, had removed the saddle in an attempt to keep him from going! As the crowd swelled, Hathorne and Corwin ordered that the questionings be moved to the meetinghouse nearby.

Sarah Good was questioned first. Hathorne accused her of making a contract with the devil, but she denied the charge. He asked why she tormented the children. She replied that she had not. Nearby, the afflicted girls made strange noises and twisted their bodies in pain. Hathorne decided to have Good held for trial.

Hathorne next questioned Sarah Osborn. Osborn argued that she had hurt no one and that the devil must be using her likeness to hurt the afflicted girls. When asked why she had stopped attending church, she answered that she had been ill for more than a year. Her husband confirmed this. Still, Hathorne decided that Osborn would face trial.

Tituba was the last to face Hathorne. After repeated questioning, she finally said that a great black dog, a tall man, and four women, including Good and Osborn, had all commanded her to join them and hurt the girls. She was placed in Salem Jail alongside the other two women to await trial.

TODAY'S PERSPECTIVE

Residents of Salem Village were alarmed by the behavior of the afflicted girls. To them, the girls' convulsions, odd postures, and strange noises were proof of an "evil hand." In attempting to understand the Salem witch trials, modern investigators have considered the possibility that the girls might have been exposed to a fungus in rye, a common ingredient in bread. Such exposure could have made them sick, explaining their odd behavior.

Other villagers were soon accused of witchcraft. Twelve-year-old Ann Putnam pointed the finger at Dorcas Good, Sarah's four-year-old daughter. She also accused Giles Corey's wife, Martha. Soon afterward, Martha was accused of witchcraft by two other villagers. She denied all accusations.

Ann Putnam next accused Rebecca Nurse's specter of attacking her. Abigail Williams claimed that she too had been visited by Nurse's specter.

The list of villagers accused of witchcraft grew steadily. Even Giles Corey soon found himself a suspect of the crime. Bridget Bishop was jailed after Ann Putnam and Mercy Lewis accused her. Abigail Williams raised charges against the Reverend George Burroughs. The villagers heard rumors that Burroughs possessed

Witchcraft trials were often based entirely on accusations, with little real evidence.

magical strength and that he had mistreated and murdered his first two wives. Others accused Captain John Alden. Often, the decision of whether to pursue an accusation or put it to rest depended on how much the accused villagers were liked by people in the community.

A FIRSTHAND LOOK AT
ANN PUTNAM'S STATEMENT AGAINST GEORGE BURROUGHS

Several of Salem's residents made sworn statements declaring Reverend George Burroughs was a witch. Ann Putnam's statement is an excellent illustration of the fear Puritan communities had of witches. See page 60 for a link to read Putnam's statement online.

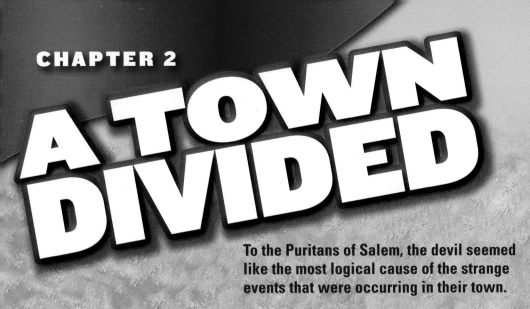

CHAPTER 2
A TOWN DIVIDED

To the Puritans of Salem, the devil seemed like the most logical cause of the strange events that were occurring in their town.

THE PURITANS BELIEVED THAT the devil constantly plotted against them. They saw evidence of that plotting all around them. Along the Maine coast, Native American warriors attacked Puritan settlements. They burned villages and killed hundreds of settlers. The colony also struggled with an outbreak of the deadly disease smallpox. In addition, Massachusetts had lost its **charter** in 1684, and Puritan minister Increase Mather had gone to England to help have it restored. To the Puritans, all of these misfortunes were the devil's work.

Colonists and Native Americans battled one another during King Philip's War in 1675 and 1676.

New England Under Attack

New England Puritans had faced threats other than witches. They remembered the horrors of King Philip's War, which had just ended in 1676. Tensions between local Native American tribes and European settlers had exploded in 1675, with Wampanoags attacking at least 25 of New England's towns. A dozen settlements were burned to the ground and many colonists were killed. The war was also fought along the Maine coast between Puritan settlers and local Abenakis. The Abenakis distrusted the settlers, who grew wealthy by selling the region's fur, fish, and timber to the Massachusetts Bay Colony. When the fighting in southern New England turned in favor of the settlers, the Wampanoags joined forces with the Abenakis. Maine's small settlements were far from one another, which made them vulnerable to attack. Many were burned, and their inhabitants were killed. The survivors fled to join relatives in Essex County, where Salem was located.

Little more than a decade after the end of King Philip's War, King William's War erupted. The Massachusetts Bay Colony was interested in reclaiming the Maine coast. As

The Abenakis became increasingly unhappy as colonists cleared land to harvest timber and build settlements.

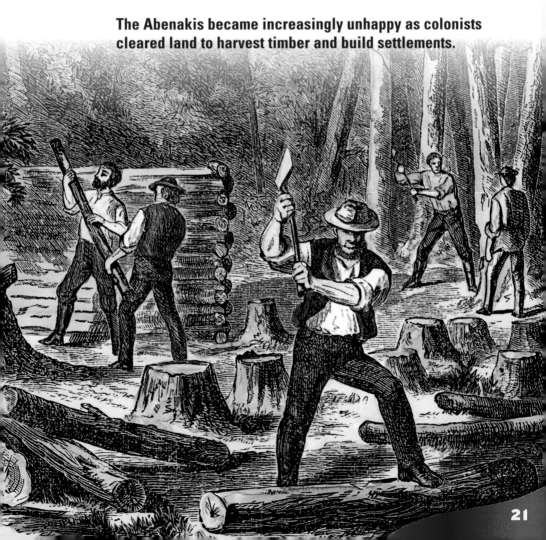

TODAY'S PERSPECTIVE

Today, some scholars suspect that many of the Maine coast refugees who relocated to Essex County likely suffered from a condition called post-traumatic stress disorder. This condition occurs in people who have witnessed horrible events, such as wars or other violence, as shown above. It can cause people to behave strangely or believe things that aren't true. Such a condition would help explain why so many people in Salem believed that they were being attacked by witches.

a result, it had given numerous land grants to men interested in resettling the region. As new towns sprang up along the coast, tensions rose and fighting began once again. Native Americans again burned coastal settlements to the ground and held the inhabitants for ransom or killed them. Once again, **refugees** fled to Essex County.

Ten of Salem's accusers, nearly two dozen of the accused, and more than a dozen judges and jurors had ties to the Maine coast. One of the refugees, Mercy Lewis, filed 54 formal legal complaints against suspected witches. Mary Walcott, who was closely related to refugees, filed 69 accusations. Often, the accusers and the accused had known each other in Maine.

For Salem's Puritans, the distinction between the Abenakis and the devil was not clear. The devil was almost always described as a dark-skinned Indian. People such as John Alden, who traded with the Abenakis, were accused of witchcraft and of having dealings with the devil. The villagers also suspected that the accused George Burroughs had formed an alliance with the Abenakis because he had escaped several raids unharmed.

A House Divided

It was unusual in the 1600s for accusations made by young girls to carry much weight. Salem's magistrates usually

The strange behavior of the young accusers convinced many adults to take their statements seriously.

ignored accusations of witchcraft. However, the girls' odd postures, strange noises, and rudeness convinced many adults that they were bewitched. As a result, magistrates found the charges believable. They were convinced that God was allowing the devil to destroy their community.

Salem was already a place divided. Salem Village had developed from Salem Town, a busy seaport, as it expanded westward. Because Salem Village was entirely within Salem Town's territory, the village did not have its own separate government. From the beginning, the village and the town charted different paths. The village

Salem Village was part of a larger area known as Salem Town, located on the Atlantic coast of Massachusetts.

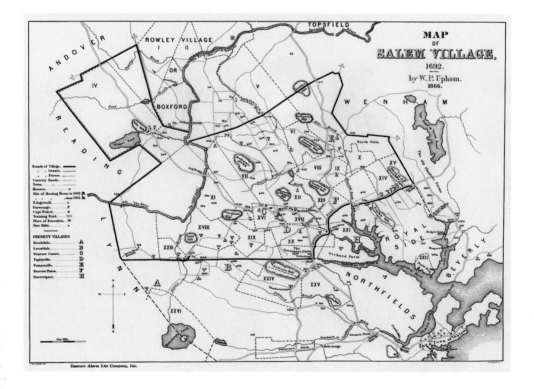

People in the western part of Salem Village lived farther from the shipping ports along the Atlantic coast than people in the eastern part of the village. Because of this, they were more likely to be farmers.

depended on farming and supplied the town with food. Villagers paid taxes to the town. However, traveling to the church in Salem Town was inconvenient for Puritans living in the village. So the village Puritans asked if they might form their own church. Town leaders would lose the taxes that villagers paid if they allowed the new church, so they refused at first.

However, the problem ran deeper than this. Farmers from the western part of the village held fast to traditional values. Those living on the east side of the village, nearer to Salem Town, were often connected to the seaport's **mercantile** interests. West village Puritans believed this threatened the entire village community.

Salem Town was home to a busy port where a wide variety of goods were traded.

A long-standing feud between two of Salem Village's major families, the Putnams and Porters, reflected the division. The Putnams lived on the western fringes of the village and were farmers. They were far from the seaport and had to depend almost solely on farming to survive. The Porters, who lived in the eastern part of the village, had many connections to the port's mercantile interests. They prospered without needing to rely on farming. As a result, the Putnams sought to gain more independence for the village, while the Porters were interested in strengthening bonds with the town and its mercantile interests. The differences that arose between the two families eventually turned into suspicions of something darker.

The family feud divided Salem Village. Some in the village's western reaches suspected that the Porters and others like them must practice magic. In the late 1600s, small books about magic practices began to be passed around Salem Village. Puritans interpreted the books as evidence that the devil had crept silently into their lives. When accusations of witchcraft began in 1692, accusers often testified that the devil had asked them to sign his little book. A large majority of the accusers lived in western Salem Village. Those accused often lived in its eastern end.

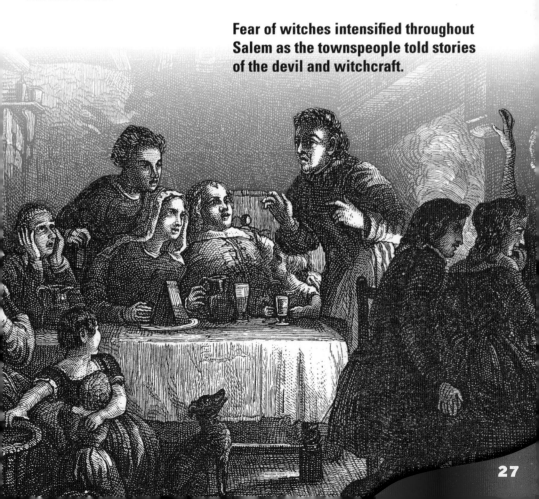

Fear of witches intensified throughout Salem as the townspeople told stories of the devil and witchcraft.

Samuel Parris (left) stirred up fear of witchcraft with his sermons, leading to the imprisonment of many people as they awaited trial.

Stirring the Pot

Reverend Parris played a central role in driving the divided community to the breaking point. When the village offered Parris a position as church minister, he stalled for several months while driving a hard bargain in reaching terms for his employment. Church officials wondered if they had chosen the right man. Despite their reservations, Parris's sermons were well attended.

His sermons, however, soon revealed his obsessions. Parris delivered several sermons that hinted at Salem Town's poor treatment of the village. Parris also spoke increasingly of threats to the church and threats from within the church.

This worried the colonists, who were already upset at changes in a new charter from England. This charter gave power over local issues to the royal governors appointed by the king of England. Local lawmakers

Disagreements were common between people from the town and people from the village.

After the 1691 charter, King William III was responsible for choosing the government leaders of Massachusetts.

were left powerless. In addition, whereas in the original charter only Puritan men were allowed to vote in

A FIRSTHAND LOOK AT

THE CHARTER OF MASSACHUSETTS BAY

The Massachusetts Charter of 1691 legally established the Province of Massachusetts Bay. It took power away from local assemblies and placed it in the hands of governors appointed by the king of England. See page 60 for a link to view the charter online.

political elections, the new charter gave the same right to Anglicans and Quakers. Puritanism would no longer be the dominant religion of the region.

Puritans were divided from within and threatened by Native Americans, Anglicans, and Quakers. On a grander scale, their worldview was threatened by large changes over which they had no control. The small, close-knit communities of the previous generation were vanishing in a world changed by trade, diversity, and the printed word. For people who believed that God was ever present in their lives, all of these things had religious explanations. Everywhere they looked, they saw evidence of the devil's plot.

A VIEW FROM ABR★OAD

Quakerism began in England in the 1650s. Quakers claimed to have a true experience of Christ without ministers, which was blasphemous to the Church of England. The upstart movement threatened to overturn social order. Despite this, the movement's popularity continued to grow. When a new law passed in 1664 threatened Quakerism's continued existence in England, many Quakers migrated to the American colonies. The movement flourished in the Delaware Valley and in Pennsylvania, and it threatened Puritan dominance in New England.

CHAPTER 3

TRIALS

Before becoming a judge, William Stoughton studied theology at Harvard College and worked as a preacher in Massachusetts.

WITH THE NUMBER OF witchcraft accusations increasing by the day, Salem had dozens of cases to hear by the time the region's new governor, Sir William Phips, arrived from England. The sheer volume of witchcraft cases overwhelmed the regular court system, so Phips created a new court to hear them. He appointed William Stoughton the new court's chief justice. Six members of Phips's council acted as judges.

Bridget Bishop was the first person to be executed during the Salem witch trials.

Dark Days

On June 2, 1692, the new court met for the first time to consider the case of Bridget Bishop. When John Hathorne had questioned Bishop on April 19, he had been unable to make her confess to witchcraft. At the June hearing, the evidence was stacked against her. She had a strange mark on her body that was believed to be a "devil's mark." The accusers claimed that Bishop's specter had pinched, choked, and bit them.

Deliverance Hobbs testified that she had seen Bishop perform witchcraft in a field with other people. A workman who had taken down a wall in Bishop's home seven years earlier testified that he had found dolls with pins sticking in them. This was taken as evidence that Bishop had used them to cast harmful magic spells on other people. Her husband had died suddenly, and she was blamed for it. What no one mentioned, but all knew, was that Bishop was widely disliked in the village because she had been harsh in business dealings. She also was from Salem Town. The jury considered her case, found her guilty, and ordered her to be hanged. The next day, a jury **indicted** John Willard and Rebecca Nurse.

The court met again at the end of June. Sarah Good and four other women—Rebecca Nurse, Sarah Wildes, Elizabeth Howe, and

Dolls like this one were believed to have magical properties.

In 1692, several types of evidence were accepted in Salem as proof of witchcraft. If a witch's victim saw the specter of the person afflicting him or her, it was considered evidence that the person had made a pact with the devil. If an afflicted person responded to an alleged witch's touch by becoming calm, it was accepted that the magic that caused the torments had been withdrawn by the accused. Telling fortunes and possessing dolls were also considered evidence of witchcraft. Many of these forms of evidence were unfair to the accused. In modern court systems, much stronger evidence is needed to prove accused criminals guilty.

Susannah Martin— were tried for crimes of witchcraft. A variety of evidence was used to convict Good. Deliverance Hobbs claimed to have seen her at the same witches' meeting that she had seen Bishop attend. Samuel and Mary Abbey, who had brought Good and her four-year-old daughter, Dorcas, into their home, now testified against her. They claimed that Good had used magic to kill their livestock after she was asked to leave. Even Dorcas said that her mother practiced witchcraft. Good protested the evidence, but she was convicted.

Rebecca Nurse was 71 years old at the time of her trial.

Guilty as Charged

Rebecca Nurse's family had collected the signatures of 39 people who all agreed that she was a good person. Nurse also argued against the accusation that a mark on her body was the devil's mark. However, several witnesses claimed to have seen her specter. Mary Walcott claimed that the specter confessed to murders. Sarah Holton claimed that her husband, Benjamin, had died as a result of a magic spell three years earlier after his pigs went into Nurse's garden. The jury at first found Nurse not guilty, but the afflicted "made a hideous outcry" at the verdict. Judge Stoughton asked the jury to reconsider the evidence. This time, they found Nurse guilty of

People convicted of witchcraft were hanged in public, drawing crowds of interested spectators.

witchcraft and sentenced her to death by hanging. Wildes, Howe, and Martin were also found guilty.

Nurse's defense raised serious questions about the reliability of considering visions of specters to be evidence. Specifically, it raised doubt in some minds as to whether the devil could command the specter of someone to torment another person. A dozen influential local ministers, including Cotton Mather of Boston, had already cautioned the court to not rely exclusively on spectral evidence. Opposition to the trials was beginning to gain ground. Still, all five accused women were hanged on July 19.

The court came together again on August 2. George Burroughs, Martha Carrier, John and Elizabeth Proctor, George Jacobs, and John Willard were all tried and found guilty. Elizabeth Proctor was pregnant at the time. She was granted a delay of execution until her baby was born. However, her husband, John, was executed with the five others on August 19. Elizabeth was never executed.

The Final Phase

The defense of Rebecca Nurse raised many valid arguments against the use of spectral evidence. Though it was generally agreed that spectral torments required other types of supporting evidence, no one argued against the use of spectral evidence until magistrate Robert Pike wrote an influential letter to justice Jonathan Corwin. Pike argued that there was no way of proving whether or not a witness had actually seen a specter, imagined it, or simply made it up.

The court met again beginning on September 6. Over the next 12 days, 15 people were indicted, and 14 stood trial. All 14 were convicted. Dorcas Hoar was tried first and convicted, based largely on the testimony of her neighbors. Hoar's husband, William, had died the previous winter. Neighbors whispered that she had caused his death. Many believed that widows were more likely to turn to witchcraft than women whose husbands were still alive. In addition, four girls testified that Hoar's specter had abused them. She was found guilty.

On Sunday, September 11, Reverend Parris delivered a memorable sermon to remind villagers how much was at stake. He spoke of their times as a battle between the devil's "army" and the followers of Christ. Parris described the devil's assaults in images that reminded the faithful of the horrors of Abenaki attacks on the northern frontier.

Over the next few days, prisoners John Alden, Edward Bishop, and Sarah Bishop escaped from jail. Now that Parris had connected witchcraft with the Abenakis, Alden knew that his practice of trading with the Indians would be enough to condemn him. He fled and went into hiding.

By September 17, only the fate of Giles Corey remained undecided. He had never confessed or agreed to a jury trial. English law required that he be punished by *peine forte et dure*, or torture. Heavy stones would be piled on him until he either agreed to a trial or died a slow death. The night before his final punishment, 12-year-old Ann Putnam claimed to have a vision of a ghost who said that Corey had murdered him years before. Some, including Ann's mother and father, had believed rumors that Corey beat a servant to death in 1675. Ann was too young to have remembered the event herself, but she was old enough to repeat stories she had heard. However, Cotton Mather claimed that Ann's vision proved God's working in the world and the truth of Ann's visions. Two days later, Giles Corey died beneath a massive stone pile.

A memorial to Giles Corey stands today in Salem, Massachusetts.

GILES COREY
PRESSED TO DEATH
SEPT. 19. 1692

CHAPTER 4

AWAKENING

Law enforcement officials often forced confessions from people accused of witchcraft.

BY THE TIME EIGHT OF THE convicted were hanged on September 22, the controversy that swirled around the trials could no longer be ignored. Six other people had confessed to stall their own executions. They promised to name other witches. Dozens of other suspects were imprisoned and awaiting trial. The province's new charter required the court to follow English law, which banned forcing confessions through torture and other methods of coercion. Despite this, these methods were commonly used during the trials.

Governor William Phips and his wife, Mary, both came under suspicion during the witch trials.

Voices of Dissent

During the September trials, Massachusetts governor William Phips traveled to Pemaquid, Maine, which had fallen to the Abenakis after an attack three years earlier. When he returned to Massachusetts, he found that public opinion about the witch trials had begun to shift. Phips also found that he and his wife were now under a cloud of suspicion. He had employed a fortune-teller, and his wife was related to a woman who had been accused of witchcraft decades earlier. While the governor was at Pemaquid, his wife ordered one of the accused witches to be released.

Things were changing quickly in Salem. The executions of September 22 were heart wrenching. Mary Easty, condemned to death by hanging, bid farewell to her family. Easty had earlier pleaded with Phips and the judges, asking that innocents be spared. She declared that many confessions had been forced. Others joined her in speaking out against the unfair evidence of the trials. Increase Mather cautioned against convicting suspects of witchcraft based on spectral evidence or

Samuel Wardwell was one of the people hanged for witchcraft on September 22.

Cotton Mather

Cotton Mather was born in Boston in 1663 to a family of well-known Puritan ministers. He entered college at the age of 12 and earned a master's degree by the time he was 18. He soon followed in the footsteps of his father, Increase Mather, and other relatives by becoming a minister. Mather quickly developed a large following, and his sermons and writings influenced many people throughout New England.

During the Salem witch trials, Mather used his influence to encourage accusations of witchcraft. Despite this, he and his father both argued against the use of spectral evidence in the trials.

touch tests alone. Reverend Samuel Willard of Boston prepared a pamphlet in support of Philip English and John Alden.

However, some people continued to support the trials. Cotton Mather wrote *The Wonders of the Invisible World* in defense of his position. Governor Phips was caught uncomfortably between the trials' supporters and opponents. He temporarily blocked publication of all writings about them. Phips also wrote a letter about the trials to the English government in London and sent more letters to other colonial governors about their processes for trying witches. While he waited for replies, dozens of jailed suspects revealed that they had been forced to confess.

Suspected witches were jailed while they awaited trial. In jail, officials often tried to get the accused to sign a confession.

Untying the Knot

The Massachusetts government had to decide what to do about the dozens of additional suspects still imprisoned. Local ministers, who had consulted with the court's

A FIRSTHAND LOOK AT
A LETTER FROM WILLIAM PHIPS TO WILLIAM BLATHWAYT

In October 1962, Governor William Phips sent a letter to London to discuss the matter of the witch trials with the English government. See page 60 for a link to read the entire letter online.

One of the judges who oversaw the witch trials apologized years later for his role in the trials.

judges during the trials, were requested to give their advice. On October 29, Phips dissolved the court that had been specially formed to oversee the witch trials. He ordered the remaining trials to be conducted by the region's regular court the following January. All but three of the remaining accused were eventually **acquitted**. Governor Phips later pardoned the three who had been convicted. The trials had finally come to an end.

Boston merchant Robert Calef, a Baptist, wrote a book during the mid-1690s that spoke out against the trials and their dark legacy, especially the role played by Cotton Mather. However, Mather's influence was so great that no colonial publisher dared to print the book. In addition, Quaker Thomas Maule criticized the Puritans' handling of the trials in a book

A VIEW FROM ABROAD

Governor Phips's letter to London was the English government's first official notification of the problems faced by the province. Phips acknowledged the horrible course the trials had taken and attempted to distance himself from them. He lied in his letter, stating that he had been absent during almost all of the trials. English law did not look kindly on forced confessions, and Phips feared that he would be punished for allowing such events to occur in Salem.

published in 1695. Maule's book pointed out that the Puritans had put many innocent people to death.

The end of the trials did not always end the problems for all of the accused. Upon acquittal, a prisoner was required to pay fees before he or she could be released. These fees were meant to cover the costs of feeding and housing prisoners. Some who were acquitted could not afford the fees. They were forced to remain in jail for many months without hope of release, and two died there. Others paid the fees but were left with almost no money to support themselves after being freed. In addition, Essex County sheriff George Corwin had seized the land of many of the people who had been hanged, denying their children rightful inheritances. The **descendants** of most of the wrongly accused were not **compensated** for their losses until December 1711.

A 1711 act cleared the names of many people who had been accused of witchcraft.

Regni *ANNÆ* Reginæ Decimo.

Province of the Maſſachuſetts-Bay.

AN ACT,

Made and Paſſed by the Great and General Court or Aſſembly of Her Majeſty's Province of the Maſſachuſetts-Bay in New-England, Held at Boſton the 17th Day of October, 1711.

An Act to Reverſe the Attainders of *George Burroughs* and others for Witchcraft.

FORASMUCH as in the Year of our Lord One Thouſand Six Hundred Ninety Two, Several Towns within this Province were Infeſted with a horrible Witchcraft or Poſſeſſion of Devils ; And at a Special Court of Oyer and Terminer holden at Salem, in the County of Eſſex in the ſame Year One Thouſand Six Hundred Ninety Two, George Burroughs of Wells, John Procter, George Jacob, John Willard, Giles Core, and his Wife, Rebecca Nurſe, and Sarah Good, all of Salem aforeſaid : Elizabeth How, of Ipſwich, Mary Eaſtey, Sarah Wild and Abigail Hobbs all of Topsfield : Samuel Wardell, Mary Parker, Martha Carrier, Abigail Falkner, Anne Foſter, Rebecca Eames, Mary Poſt, and Mary Lacey, all of Andover : Mary Bradbury of Saliſbury : and Dorcas Hoar of Beverly ; Were ſeverally Indicted, Convicted and Attained of Witchcraft, and ſome of them put to Death, Others lying ſtill under the like Sentence of the ſaid Court, and liable to have the ſame Executed upon them.

A   The

In 2001, Massachusetts governor Jane Swift cleared the names of five witches who had been convicted and hanged during the Salem witch trials.

Five of the executed witches were not included in the 1711 law to provide compensation. There was no recognition that they had been innocent and wrongly put to death. Their descendants protested. Finally, in 2001, Massachusetts governor Jane Swift officially declared their innocence, more than 300 years after their deaths. It was the only gesture left to try to correct the awful events of the trials.

What Happened Where?

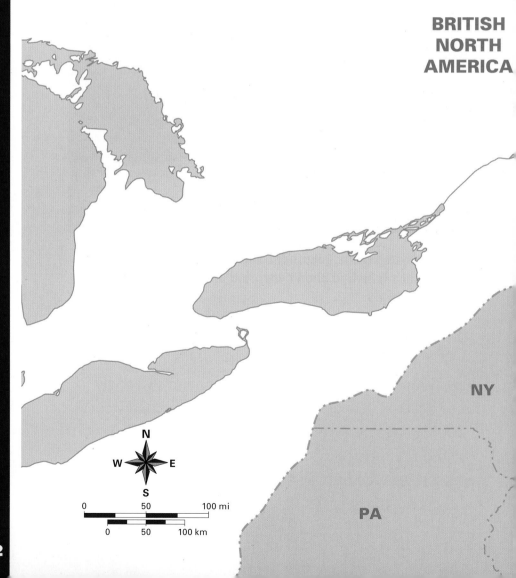

BRITISH
NORTH
AMERICA

NY

PA

N
W E
S

0   50   100 mi

0   50   100 km

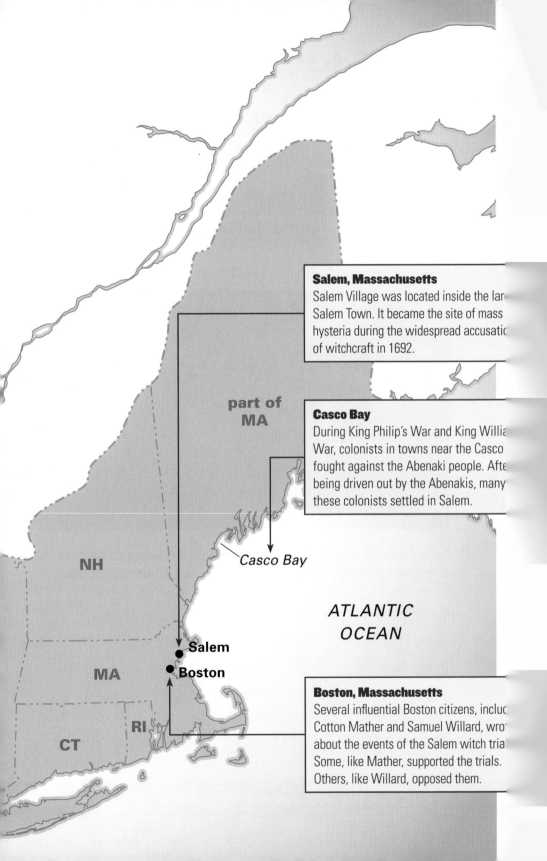

Salem, Massachusetts
Salem Village was located inside the lar[ge]
Salem Town. It became the site of mass
hysteria during the widespread accusati[ons]
of witchcraft in 1692.

part of MA

Casco Bay
During King Philip's War and King Willia[m's]
War, colonists in towns near the Casco
fought against the Abenaki people. Afte[r]
being driven out by the Abenakis, many
these colonists settled in Salem.

Casco Bay

NH

ATLANTIC OCEAN

Salem
Boston

MA

RI

CT

Boston, Massachusetts
Several influential Boston citizens, includ[ing]
Cotton Mather and Samuel Willard, wro[te]
about the events of the Salem witch tria[ls.]
Some, like Mather, supported the trials.
Others, like Willard, opposed them.

Today, court trials require much stronger evidence to convict accused criminals than they did during the Salem witch trials.

The Salem witch crisis has had a lasting influence on American history. The modern world is very different from the world of 1692. It might be difficult to imagine accusations of witchcraft being taken seriously today. However, the troubles caused by suspicions and unfounded accusations that shaped the trials did not disappear.

The term *witch hunt* is still used to describe situations that recall the Salem crisis. One of the best-known witch hunts in recent history took place in 1953, when Senator Joseph McCarthy launched investigations of suspected **communists**. As panic spread across the United States, people began to suspect countless innocent people of being communists. Like the accused witches of Salem, many people were forced to defend themselves in court against unfair charges.

More than three centuries have passed since the Salem witch trials, but this horrific event still holds valuable lessons. For the courts, it is a reminder of the importance of fair trials and high standards for evidence. To the rest of the world, it is a cautionary tale about the destructive power of jealousy and anger.

Senator Joseph McCarthy (standing) led a modern-day "witch hunt" against people he suspected of being communists.

THE U.S. STATE DEPARTMENT OF COMMUNIS

William Phips

John Alden (?–1701) was a successful merchant with strong ties to the Maine frontier. He was accused of witchcraft and jailed, but escaped and survived the ordeal.

Increase Mather (1639–1723) was the father of Cotton Mather, a Puritan minister, ambassador, and chief negotiator of the province's new charter. He and his son urged caution in the use of spectral evidence at trials.

John Hathorne (1641–1717) was an investigator and judge during the early examinations of suspected witches.

William Phips (1651–1693) was governor of Massachusetts under the province's new charter. He helped bring an end to the witch trials in October 1692.

George Burroughs (ca. 1652–1692) was a Puritan minister with ties to the Abenakis in Maine. He was accused of witchcraft, tried, and executed.

Samuel Parris (1653–1720) was a controversial Puritan minister in Salem Village. His sermons divided the settlement and energized Salem's witch hysteria.

Cotton Mather (1663–1728) was an influential Boston Puritan minister and a vocal supporter of the witch trials.

Samuel Parris

Ann Putnam (1679–1716) was the 12-year-old daughter of Thomas Putnam and Ann Carr Putnam. Fifty-three legal complaints of witchcraft were filed on her behalf.

Abigail Williams (1680–?) was the niece of Reverend Samuel Parris. She and Parris's daughter Elizabeth (1682–1760) were afflicted, and their complaints helped begin the long string of witchcraft accusations in Salem.

Cotton Mather

TIMELINE

1675–1676

King Philip's War is waged.

1684

Massachusetts loses its charter.

1692

January
Elizabeth Parris and Abigail Williams appear bewitched.

March 12
Martha Corey is accused of witchcraft.

April
John Hathorne attempts to force Bridget Bishop to confess to witchcraft.

May
The new charter arrives in Massachusetts; a special court is created to hear the witch trials.

June 2
The court meets for the first time.

June 10
Bridget Bishop, the first convicted witch, is hanged.

Late June
The second session of the court begins.

1688-1697

King William's War takes place.

1689

Samuel Parris is hired as a Puritan minister in Salem Village.

1692 (continued)

August
The third session of the court begins; five colonists convicted of witchcraft are executed.

September
The fourth session of the court begins; more colonists convicted of witchcraft are executed.

October 12
Governor Phips writes to the English government in London about the witch trials.

October 29
Governor Phips dissolves the court, ending all witch trials.

1711

December
Descendants of the wrongly accused are compensated.

LIVING HISTORY

Primary sources provide firsthand evidence about a topic.
Witnesses to a historical event create primary sources. They
include autobiographies, newspaper reports of the time, oral
histories, photographs, and memoirs. A secondary source
analyzes primary sources and is one step or more removed from
the event. Secondary sources include textbooks, encyclopedias,
and commentaries. To view the following primary and secondary
sources, go to www.factsfornow.scholastic.com. Enter the keywords
Salem Witch Trials and look for the Living History logo Σ¡.

Σ¡ Ann Putnam's Statement Against George Burroughs

The Reverend George Burroughs was one of many Salem
residents accused of witchcraft. Ann Putnam's official statement
against him provides an excellent example of the types of charges
that were raised against innocent people during the witch trials.

Σ¡ The Arrest Warrant for Elizabeth Proctor and Sarah Cloyce

On August 2, 1692, Salem residents Elizabeth Proctor
and Sarah Cloyce were tried for witchcraft. The warrant issued for
their arrest was typical of the time. It accused the two women of
committing witchcraft against a variety of other Salem villagers.

Σ¡ The Charter of Massachusetts Bay

The Massachusetts
Charter of 1691 legally established the Province of Massachusetts
Bay. It took power away from local lawmakers and provided
people of non-Puritan religions with more rights. This angered the
Puritans, as it challenged their authority in the area.

Σ¡ A Letter from William Phips to William Blathwayt

Massachusetts governor William Phips sent a letter to London,
England, in October 1692 to inform the English government of the
witch trials' status. In it, he mentions that the arrests have finally
been put on hold.

RESOURCES

Books

Benoit, Peter. *The British Colonies in North America*. New York: Children's Press, 2013.

Fradin, Judith Bloom, and Dennis Brindell Fradin. *The Salem Witch Trials*. Tarrytown, NY: Marshall Cavendish, 2009.

Hinman, Bonnie. *The Massachusetts Bay Colony: The Puritans Arrive from England*. Hockessin, DE: Mitchell Lane, 2007.

Nardo, Don. *The Salem Witch Trials*. Detroit: Lucent, 2007.

Slavicek, Louise Chipley. *The Salem Witch Trials: Hysteria in Colonial America*. New York: Chelsea House, 2011.

Waxman, Laura Hamilton. *Who Were the Accused Witches of Salem? And Other Questions About the Witchcraft Trials*. Minneapolis: Lerner Publications, 2012.

Visit this Scholastic Web site for more information on the Salem witch trials: www.factsfornow.scholastic.com Enter the keywords Salem Witch Trials

GLOSSARY

acquitted (uh-KWIT-id) found not guilty of a crime

afflictions (uh-FLIK-shuhnz) things that cause suffering

charter (CHAHR-tur) a formal document that states the rights or duties of a group of people, or that creates an institution such as a company or a university

communists (KAHM-yuh-nists) people who believe that all the land, property, businesses, and resources belong to the government or community, and that the profits should be shared by all

compensated (KOM-puhn-sate-id) repaid for the value of lost property

descendants (di-SEN-duhnts) your descendants are your children, their children, and so on into the future

indicted (in-DITE-id) officially charged with a crime

inheritance (in-HER-uh-tuhns) money or property from someone who has died

magistrates (MAJ-uh-strates) government officials who can act as judges in court

mercantile (MUR-kuhn-tyl) having to do with the buying and selling of goods

ministers (MIN-uh-sturz) people who lead religious ceremonies in church

refugees (REF-yoo-jeez) people who are forced to leave their homes or countries to escape war, religious persecution, or a natural disaster

sermon (SUR-muhn) a speech given during a religious service

specter (SPEK-tur) a ghost or phantom

INDEX

Page numbers in *italics* indicate illustrations.

ABOUT THE AUTHOR

Peter Benoit earned a degree in mathematics at Skidmore College. He is an educator and poet. He has written more than four dozen books for Scholastic/Children's Press on topics including disasters, Native Americans, ecosystems, the *Titanic*, the electoral college, and the 2012 election. He has also written several books on crucial moments in American history, and books on ancient Greece and ancient Rome. Benoit is a student of colonial America. He lives in Greenwich, New York.